EARLY POEMS

BY

M. A.

LONDON
ELKIN MATHEWS, CORK STREET
1913

CONTENTS

POEMS

Contents

IRREGULAR SONNETS

Contents

POEMS

QUO VADIS?

THE lane winds on below the hill,
  Beside the wood, across the plain,
The way is rough, the ruts are deep,
    And full of rain.

The sunset floods the long wet road,
The tangled grass, the pebbles bright,
The soft gray mud, and turns the ruts
    To lines of light.

Against the sky with stretching arms,
And slightly bent, with beckoning hands,
With lichen moss on rotting wood,
    A sign-post stands.

The Castle of the Poppies

THE CASTLE OF THE POPPIES

ACROSS the jagged mountain lands,
Beyond the shores and shaken strands,
The Castle of the Poppies stands.

Among the strange fantastic trees,
Which throw slight shadowy traceries
Along its walls and terraces,

It stands amid the crimson flowers,
Which hang tall grown like weeping showers,
Thro'out the sleepy summer hours.

'Tis silent as a place of tombs;
Few dwellers move within its rooms;
Only across the twilight glooms

There steals the strain of melodies
Along the poppied terraces,
And thro' the suffocating trees.

The poppies droop towards the sun
In heavy mantles one by one,
Until the cruel day is done.

Their purple pollen with the dusk
Is wafted through the air like musk,
And mingled with the poppy-husk.

The Castle of the Poppies

It blinds the eyes and dulls the brain,
Compels the soul like one in pain,
Who dreams but may not rise again.

*   *   *   *   *

The seven rivers girdle wide
The Poppy Castle every side,
And wander down towards the tide.

Their streams are crimson with the blood
Of poppies blown across the wood,
And past the sunless solitude.

The petals travel to the sea,
(For they are lost and fallen free,)
Lightly and very joyously.

But round the castle no foot falls;
Only a wood-bird loudly calls,
Whilst thro' the measured intervals

The poppies bloom and fall apace
Across the castle's furrowed face,
Battered by blows in many a place.

The towers and the turrets glow
Through each red sunset, while below
The poppies murmur to and fro.

The petals of the poppies lie
Like red wine spillèd wantonly;
Like shuddering fires against the sky,

The Castle of the Poppies

They twine about the castle tall,
Filling the crannies of the wall,
Luring the stones to shake and fall.

They hang about the mullioned gate,
Like the strong bloody hands of Fate
Which hold the spirit desolate.

They clutch the towers and compel
The living dead, who therein dwell
To hold dark colloquies with Hell!

*　　*　　*　　*　　*

The Idler of the Dusk who strays
Along the sombre forest ways,
Amid the throbbing amber days,

Shall meet the pollen floating by,
Which dulls the soul and dims the eye,
So that alone and fearfully,

He wanders there with callous brain,
Like one who falls asleep for pain,
And dreams, but dares not rise again.

THE KNIGHTS' LITANY

HERE lies Alan de Fitzwight,
A gallant true and lovelie knight,
And Dame Mirabelle his wife.

The Knights' Litany

Here lies Everard de Ros,
Whose life was grief and bitter loss,
And Lady Rosalis his wife.

Here lies also Gilbert de Gant,
To whom Christ shall fitlie grant
Everlasting truth and life.

And Orm of Heletune a Knight,
Whose deeds to all time shall give light;
And Lady Flavia his bliss.

Here lies Liulph de Lumlie dead,
Whose faire blood was vilelie shed,
Cross them piously who read.

Peter de Maulie here too lies,
Whose faire fame no man may despise;
For his wife Alice tell thy beads.

Here lies Sir Hugh de Heddlestone,
Whose golden spurs were knightlie won;
Here sleeps Heloise his wife.

Here lies Christopher de Lym,
A dragon was well slain by him,
Gold-haired maidens dream of this.

Here lies John of Jarrow, he
Who sailed across the mightie sea
Unto the City of the Lord.

The Knights' Litany

In the spirit-stirring quiet,
When ye leave all stir and riot,
Saints and Poets pray for us.

From our helmets the red rust
Stains each shield with copper dust,
And our crests grow gray and faint.

And the shadows without sound
Darken gold or argent ground,
Or the pious Pelican.

Silver star and crescent moon,
Above the Lords of Heletune,
On the sable face of night.

Golden lilies three and three,
Above the Knights of Valerie,
On an azure of the field.

Ribbed and fluted chalices,
Filled with wine of Jesu's peace,
Above Sir Gui de Montemar,

By stainèd windows red and blue,
The pallid twilight streameth thro',
Upon our everlasting shade.

See our shields grow not too dim;
Round the holy throne of Him
We do watch ye at your prayers.

The Knights' Litany

With our hands crossed on our breast
Lie we straight and take our rest,
Goodly deeds be our repose.

Envoi
So read I in the stirring quiet,
Far from pain and bitter riot;
Saints and Poets pray for me!

A PILGRIMAGE OF SORROW

TO the jewel-like pools and the flowered woods,
He came from the shadowless solitudes,
And high on his helmet a sapphire flame,
Burnt like the light of undying fame.

He passed in a posture burdened with woe,
By favoured ways where his steed would go,
Like one grown old in a shadow of sorrow,
Gray-hearted and sick at the thought of the morrow.

Slow and sad like a soul in pain,
Bound by the dream of a love-crazed brain,
Who may not breathe with a careless breast,
For the shroud that lies on his murdered rest.

His lips were sad with the songs of those
Who sing their sorrow for lovers' repose:
Passionate poets, whose passion unsaid,
Is sung for love's balm, when the singers are dead.

A Pilgrimage of Sorrow

His face was keen as the winds of even
Blown over star-strewn seas of Heaven,
And the depths of his eyes were swift and free,
Like the windy wastes of a summer sea.

His eyes were awide with the dreams of them,
Whose deaths be sung like a requiem;
And the tears which fell from his throbbing soul
Glowed to an opal aureole.

Fretted and flushed from the fever of love,
With brows left pure from the passion thereof.

He rode where the stars grew thick in the grass,
Shivering to fire where his steed did pass,
While the blossomed trees, with glittering gems,
Swayed to and fro from their slender stems;

While the flushed wet blooms of the springing year,
Tossed their dews in an amorous fear,
And the faint Moon-blossom deserted her lover,
To moan in the deep moss canopied over.

And the lakes grew lurid with fond despair,
And ached at sight of a thing so fair,
And called to the wind with a passionate grace
To blind their eyes from sight of his face.

And the spring leaves felt that the autumn had come,
Tho' the woods were hushed and the waters dumb,

A Pilgrimage of Sorrow

And fell around him like glowing rain
Blown on to a sunset window-pane;

And turned to amber and gold and red,
And showers of silver silently shed,
Like the flame of a soul on a windless sky
Burning starward and Godward fervently,

And lay on his heart in a sensuous trance,
And sighed in voluptuous dalliance,
With the heat of a soul made free of the flesh,
With sense untinged and passion afresh.

Till they sank like the sighs of a sick desire
When love dies down and the lamps expire.

And the breezes pined with the wish to give:
The sweetness of life, as we love and live,
And blew with the scent of a tidal sea,
Givers of gifts given lavishly.

And the rude weeds sprang from below his feet,
Flushed into flame at a form so sweet,
Firing with colour, while sudden wine
Gushed from the roots of the columbine.

But he passed them by like a heart in sorrow,
All solitary-souled for the thought of the morrow.

And the love of many a fire-dipped bud
Sank down to the slough and was lost in mud,
Where the hoofs of his steed with no thought for pain
Trampled the sod where their love had lain.

11

A Pilgrimage of Sorrow

For lyrical ecstasies rang in his ears,
Of faiths forlorn and unperished biers,
And the sheen of his lance was a wand of white,
Shining alone like a lost delight.

And above him the clouds grew still in the sky,
Like the hush of a chorused minstrelsy,
And the distant country seen thro' the leaves
Was blue with the blue of a hundred eves.

And the spirits of grace in the twilight air
Sighed for want of a soul so fair,
And the spirits of those who have died of love,
Murmured and moved in the dusk above.

And the spirits of forest and pool and plain
Sighed for a night and a day in vain,
For the souls of the lovers and poets afar,
Were shown like the gleam of a golden star.

And softly by threads of a silvery silk,
Soft as the flavour of magic milk,
Sweet as the songs of enchanted streams
Which once have watered the garden of dreams.

They stole his soul from the jewelled woods,
And the gray-streaked shadowless solitudes;

They drugged his spirit from aching sorrow,
From horror of thought and the fear of the morrow,
And the tears which fell from his soaring soul
Clothed him around with an aureole.

Song

SONG

OH take thy lips and hands away,
    The lips that burn, the hands that bless:
Lest all the body and the soul
    Should swoon away from tenderness.

Ah leave thy hands around me still,
    And set thy lips where these shall be,
That all the body and the soul
    Be blessed unto eternity!

Ah give to me thy lips and hands,
    Thy lips that burn, thy hands that bless!
Till all the body and the soul
    Shall swoon away from tenderness.

THE ORCHARD-CLOSE

LINGERING in the orchard-close
    In the angry dawn,
Where I saw your little house,
    O my Lady!

Desolated and forlorn,
Leaning on the wall,
Red as heart's blood was the morn,
    Dark and cloudy.

The Orchard-Close

Cherry blossoms fall and shine
Whiter than the snow,
Hiding yellow celandine,
    O my Lady!

If I laid me lying low
All beneath the tree,
Would they hide me sleeping so,
    O my Lady?

Would you hear them suddenly
Falling fast and fast,
Till they reached the heart of me,
    Dark and cloudy?

Would you, stepping forth at last
To your orchard-close,
See me as you wandered past,
    O my Lady?

SONG OF THE VIRGINAL ISLES

SCATTER the stars down into the eyes!
    Shatter the moon-globe over the soul,
Drench the spirit with moonlit waters:
Rites baptismal over the soul!
Plague and entice with the moon's white daughters;
Shake the star-dust into the eyes,
Blind them and bind them and bid them die
To all but the gold lakes of Paradise,

Song of the Virginal Isles

And silvery phantoms that go thereby!
Shed the sunset over the heart,
Drench it in crimson and gold and sheen,
With melodic passion and sensuous smart,
Like faint dream kisses which never have been!
Fling the rainbow into the eyes,
Enslave the soul with a melancholy,
Melancholy tender, mellow and wise,
Of maidenly motion languid and holy.
Shed the magical ways of the west,
Which carpet the shoreless echoing sea,
Far over the spirit, deep into the breast,
So the wild sea-sandals be given to me!
So that we tread on the ripples of fire
Which flow from the sunset and go to the moon,
Which sing like the hymn of a murmuring wire,
Fearful itself of its magical tune!
Let us go by the gold-dusted plains of the sea,
To Virginal Islands in spaces unfound,
Where taintless foam washes untrammelled and free
Over the fresh cold blossoming ground.
Where flowers are nameless, of colours unknown,
With odours undreamed of, and perilous hues:
Tawny wild yellows of soul-drunken tone,
Crimsons unsparing, and rapturous blues.
Where the long leaves are living and chant with low
      moans
To the chorus of streams running over the moss,
Their musical garrulous undertones,   .

Song of the Virginal Isles

Of sweet-hearted pities and love-honoured loss.
Where deep flame-ambers flow over the woods,
Fiery and rare and crystalline clear,
Filling the odorous solitudes
With sounds that are distant and scents which are near.
Till the dusk of the Island dies down to a dream,
And hushed tame senses drink deep of the dew,
And the murmur of many a garrulous stream
Spreads over the passions a pleasure anew.
A pleasure made out of the feverless dells
Pale with star-blossoms and heavy with night,
Mild with the musical faint moon-bells
Shining by glows of their moon-stolen light.
A pleasure made out of the passionless seas
Foaming on shores of the Virginal Isles,
Whose spray is the rhythm of rhapsodies
Filling with music the choristered miles.
Ah, come by the magical ways of the west
Flung over the passion-tossed echoing sea!
Which lead to the waters where soul-laden quest
And searching is changed into harmony.
Where the stars have myriad silver-sweet strings
Which trail on the grass and encumber with gems
The ruby rock-moss, and all the wide wings
Of golden Isle-bees with flecked diadems.
Where the dew from the moon-fields floats down to
      the earth,
And changes from wan and delirious care,
The pulse of the dusk-tides to amorous mirth,

Song of the Virginal Isles

That passion be theirs and possession so near.
So scatter the star-shine into the eyes!
Bind them and blind them and bid them see
Naught but the fire-strewn water that lies
Over the pale flooding plains of the sea!
Scatter the stars down into the eyes!

INVOCATION

SEEK not the pilgrim dole
   Thou love-anointed soul,
But come to mine abode
  O flame of God!

Set thy pure passion free;
Love and love's rhapsody,
Love and love's rapture sweet
  Shall stay thy feet.

Throughout the gilded hours
Shine the acacia flowers,
Lo, love is white as these
  Bejewelled trees.

Set thy pure passion free,
That love as red may be
As poppy fields that sweep
  The long hill-steep.

Invocation

Thou art the afterlight,
The silent handed night
Who lighteth the white star
  That burns afar!

Thou art the rustling leaves
About the morning eaves,
Thou art the melancholy
  Of the wind's cry.

The incense of the musk
Which stealeth thro' the dusk,
The evening amethyst
  Hid in the mist.

The lilies in the dew,
Stained to a copper hue
By sunset thro' the trees.
  Lo! thou art these!

*   *   *   *

Thou art the furtive theme
Haunting a waking dream,
Hid in the boundary deep
  Of life and sleep.

The vast unspoken fire
Of vagabond desire,
That knows no human home
  Where it shall come.

Invocation

I may not know nor see
Thy soul's infinity,
Yet come to mine abode,
Sweet flame of God!

TO A FRIEND

FRIEND, shall I weave thee pansies for thine ease?
Gold-bright like amber, nourished in the cool
Spring-flushed belovèd woods, and dew-lit leas,
And vapours of the jasper-hearted pool;
Or strew crushed woodbine for thy lover's peace?

Friend, from a harvest of gold gatherings
Beside full rivers of the after-rain,
What vintage shall be thine from this domain?
From blue-gray evening fields what garnerings
Shall be thine own for comfort or for gain?

Luring the flame-men from the meadow-marsh
With lutes in spring? When all the marigolds
Like scattered golden coinage fleck and splash
The emerald moist grass, and stream-banks cold
And humid from the mills' unwearied wash.

Or shall melodious twilights in the ways
Where odorous crimson apples faintly shine,
Calm violet dusks of charity be thine?
And prayer-like pauses in vexatious days
Beside some still and lily-laden shrine.

To a Friend

Quiet almond-orchards petal-strewn and sweet,
Where lingers the long clear gold-dusted gloom,
Where opalescent skies and blossoms meet,
Till twilight stars entangle with the bloom,
And fallen stars lie scattered round the feet.

Friend, shall I weave these stars to broideries,
With gracious tears and glad-souled gratitudes
For love's submissions and sweet servitudes?
For wisdom's ways and faith's divinities,
And lantern lights in desert solitudes?

THE NAMELESS ROAD

WHEN shall I find the nameless road
     And wander to the castle gate?
Passing beneath the ruined arch
   As the sweet day is growing late.

And mount the stairway of the Keep
   To find our lily garden there,
And roses and the clematis,
   As in the olden years as fair.

The cloudy musk and purple thyme,
   "Love in the Mist" and "Shade of Glen."
The narrow paths of shattered brick
   Grown over with shy cyclamen.

20

The Nameless Road

And lay me in this garden-close,
  Watching the way the twilight falls
Across the little hilly town,
  With its red roofs and battled walls.

And see the red-robed brethren come,
  Along the road that wanders down
Beside the tall gray monastery,
  And climbs towards the hilly town.

And watch the sea below the hill,
  Where the dark vessels from the south
Flee with high prows before the night,
  To rest within the harbour mouth.

And see the minstrels idle by
  With scarlet shoon and hose of brown,
The faint blue smoke arise and drift
  Across the red roofs of the town.

And lay my lips against the flowers,
  Praying their holy dew to press
Its sanctity on my desire,
  To ease me of my weariness.

Till thro' the laden twilight time,
  Veiling the silent ways of sleep,
Thy weary footfall on the stair,
  Mounts up the gray embattled Keep.

The Nameless Road

And I behold thee as a dream,
  With wonder nor with questioning,
As one who comes to blessèd lands
  After long years of languishing.

And watch thee loose thy helm and shield,
  Lay down the burden of thy sword
By the white lilies blessed and named
  Of the sweet Mother of the Lord.

Ah, kneel beside me on the musk,
  And set thy lips against my palms!
Whilst thro' the heavy-hearted dusk
  Drifts the faint chanting of the psalms.

And as the star above the sea
  Brings home the vessels from the South,
Gather my head between thy hands
  And lay thy lips upon my mouth!

O DESIDERIUM

WHAT wizard fancies bite like living fire
    Upon the dewless dawn of my desire?
  What flames of wingèd fervours bring to me
  Languor and love and passion's purity?
Behold the golden rivers flow like fire
Beyond this lampless unbeheld desire!
  They wander through the roadless vales of spring
  With strong sweet tunes and sacred shuddering,

O Desiderium

Along the moonless ways where men must go
With numbered footsteps pitiful and slow,
    Past the world's roaring and the city ways
    Whose stones are worn by many lives and days,
Where the tall houses gape with hollow eyes
Grown gaunt and thin with wisdom overwise,
    Past dead men's rooms whose walls are fallen in,
    Witness of too deep love or too great sin;
Past the low alley ways, and out again
Flooding purple stretches of the plain.

Ah, flaming floods like sunset tides aspiring
Drowning all time in unassuaged desiring!
    Languid, like amber, glowing to the sea,
    Strong as great passion's vital purity.
Who shall impute to such wild water-ways
The heavy torpor of undreaming days?
    Behold, love is like crimson or gold wines
    Or bruisèd purple grapes on twisted vines;
Like red-brown sun-enamoured amphorae
In ruined temples by the sapphire sea,
    Where roses of the east spill blooms forlorn
    Like palpitating pulses of the morn;
Some dream begotten garden of the dusk
With aromatic trees and tinctured musk,
    Some star-strewn fountain by faint palaces
    Where dwell Lost Gods and Feverish Phantasies;
Forsaken cities where the hill-winds swing
Across the yellow blossoms of the spring.

O Desiderium

Behold sweet love is some enchanted mood
Dreamed out alone amid a multitude;
    Like the heart's longing and the soul's despair,
    Or fond old tales adorable and fair;
Like a strange frenzy of the summer time
Crazy with colour, drunk with tragic rhyme;
    Like spirits of mesmeric silver seas
    Withholding passion in tense ecstasies,
Held in strong leashes till the midnight wind
Roams hollow eyed and wails for loves unsinned,
    Whose sighing and whose songs pass audibly,
    Above the shaken jaspers of the sea.
Ah, golden rivers full of flame and fire
Filling the dusk and dewtime of desire.
    Drowning the straining voices of the sea
    In denser tumult of love's purity,
Stilling the drifting waters of the west
Into a strange monotony of rest.

Broad golden rivers in the sunset air
Guiding the dawn and drooping of despair,
    Between the sundown and the morning moon
    Shall dreamful sleep be reawakened soon?
Beyond the sun-dawn and the setting star
Sleep shall be blessed as the belovèd are.
    Upon the ashen coming of the day
    Gray life shall drive love's multitudes away,
And flowing rivers languidly expire,
Beyond the rise and setting of desire.

O Desiderium

Songs sháll be learnt within love's easeful sleep
    Whereat we dreaming smile, and waking weep
That life so lightly lose a magic rhyme
Beneath the oblivion of the ways of Time.
    Sweet sleep shall tell us soulful melodies
    Brought from the Home of Secret Harmonies,
Where love may lie in passionless respite
Beyond the lure and longing of delight.

Between the moontime and the morning dew
Is love not pitiful because of you?
    Is joy not stricken like a murdered thing
    Thro' all love's wild and wilful murmuring?
Between the first dew and the risen sun
Are not young life and death become as one?
    Between the noonday and the evening dew
    Are dreams not merciful because of you?
Ah, golden rivers flowing into fire
Between the dawn and twilight of desire,
    Between the dewtime and the moonless night
    Love's languor shall become a waste delight.
Ah, deep flame rivers flowing into gold,
Laden with fevers new and fervours old,
    Long river roads which carry beyond sight
    All the derisions of the laggard night,
Love's vagabond desiring flowing free,
Like flowers of foam upon the swinging sea.

Between the shadows and their lengthening
There is not any rest for wayfaring,

O Desiderium

There is not any end to pain for us
  Whose eyes are waxen tired and tremulous;
There is not any peace for passion's beat
Nor any shelter for wind-driven feet.
  Behold we may not rise and singing go,
  Our hands are weary and our sight is slow;
Our loves are broken and our faith is cold,
The fervour of the spirit groweth old.
  The soul is torn and strangled at the birth
  By all the ways and voices of the earth.
There is no soul with whom to wander free
By grief forsaken, sure of amity.
  We are become a part of loneliness
  Like formless phantoms in a wilderness,
Thro' love and all the purity of love
Thro' passion's pain, and all the tears thereof.

Belovèd is our dream-tranquillity
Since we sought Silence in the place of thee;
  Yet break and bend us in our languishing
  By all love's wild and wayward murmuring.
Thy molten waves are good, our souls are strong,
Thy waters glow like wine and merge to song;
  Thy wounds are holy and thy blows are well,
  And all thy tortures are desirable.
We are not weak enough, nor have we wept
For life is left alone while love has slept,
  Take us and break us down O Sainted Love
  With all thine anguish and the ways thereof!

26

O Desiderium

Give us warm love or bid us droop and die
Between the bare earth and the barren sky!
   Sweep us and whirl us to the bitter sea,
   Drive us by fire or drown us utterly,
Until our blood shall flood like living light
With unrelinquished heavy-eyed delight.

Till Man confess that Love is pure like fire
For all the clamorous discords of desire.

MERCHANDISE

BARTER for my merchandise!
   Rare and secret merchandise:
Carven jades and beaten gold,
Peacocks with hard ruby eyes,
Amethysts and emeralds old.
Follow me across the sea
In the treasure-laden ships,
While the foam flies lawlessly
In the eyes across the lips,
   Barter for my merchandise!

Seek the sun-enamelled sails
Golden on the sapphire sea,
Bearing crimson cedar bales,
Silk and mellowed ivory.
While beyond the twilight fall
Copper sunsets grow and wane,

Merchandise

In a long ship straight and tall
Follow me across the main.
   Barter for my merchandise!

Where like phosphorescent wine
Gushing over moonlit bows
The long dripping weeds entwine
Round the sphinx-head at the prows.
Where the gilt-scaled dragons glimmer,
And the great snakes of the sea
Subtly twist and subtly shimmer
Follow fast and cunningly.
   Barter for my merchandise!

In the cold light of the morn,
Thro' the surging of the spray,
Shuddering like a soul forlorn
In the swift leap and the sway;
O'er the emerald-hearted sea,
Where the homeless sea-beasts go,
Krakens old despairingly
Roam the gray wastes to and fro.
   Follow for my merchandise!

Barter well, if thou shouldst find
The sea-witches, with thy gold,
For a fair sea and the wind
And the true tides costly sold.
Buy the omen of the bells

Merchandise

For the midnight and the storm,
Buy the secret of the spells
For the fear of the Sö Orm!
   Follow then my merchandise!

Till we cross the western day
To the People of the Isles,
Where they wait on wharf and way
Gazing o'er forsaken miles,
One by one from tower and town,
Trellised gate and flowery lea,
Silently they wander down
To the sea wharfs and the sea,
   Barter for my merchandise!

There the People stand and pray
Like a holy ritual blest,
Hazy in the amber day
Sinking to the glowing west.
And with prayers and piety
Bring us safe and sweetly home,
From the sea-spells and the sea,
And the flowing leagues of foam,
   Barter for my merchandise!

ODE TO PHANTASIES

DIM retinues of star-wrought Phantasies:
   The poppy laden spirits of the dusk,
Enfold the soul with ministering charities.

Ode to Phantasies

Their dustless feet are quiet, their hands bring
    Light fragile petals flushed and odorous,
From blossom-powdered valleys of the spring.

They have brought moon enchanted silences
    Which fall upon the soul like fluted tales
Of murmuring tarns, in mountain mysteries.

They have brought fabulous amulets and rings
    Of carven imageries and fables dead,
Wrought with a lost device of vanished kings.

And ruby-dust and sombre jewelries
    Of large-eyed demons of enchanted nights,
And magic metres of old poesies.

Their brows are tranquil with the calm of dreams;
    The purple light of their slight lanterns sway
Like water-weeds in opalescent streams.

Their yielding torches shudder in the wind,
    Like the sweet loves of over-laden souls
Tossed by the budding fervours of the mind.

Their words are untaught melodies, their eyes
    Are blinded by the wandering stars of night
Which robber winds have blown from paradise.

They are dream-tossed desires made free of pain,
    Or moonlit hollows in a place of shade,
Where pity-haunted amities have lain.

Ode to Phantasies

Lo, all their ways are melody, no pain
  Is brought by sound of them, no arrowed speech
Which falls upon the heart like scorching rain.

They are soul-silences of love which seem
  The after-peace of passion, and the hushed
Faint music dawning from a broken dream.

Love-laden eyelids which most sweetly close
  Inert and tranquil with the sleep of love
Upon eternities of deep repose.

They are like richly woven calm designs
  Of some tremendous hopeless happening.
Or like gold torch-light shed on purple wines

Which shake in chalices of beaten gold
  Or ringing glasses tall and ruby-red.
Or like soul-laden lyrics quaint and old

Left by the torrent of some passionate mind
  Made pure thro' passion and desire and loss,
Whose pilgrimage leaves Loveliness behind.

For later men to wonder on and see,
  And pray to, like the missal of a saint
Blazoned with vision and kept sacredly.

Interludes

INTERLUDES

SHALL God who made the blessèd day,
    Be witness of our love and say:
"Love is brief and shall not stay."
    God is blind and may not see.
    Miserere Domine.

Shall He Who made the secret night,
Love's desire and love's delight,
Bid the bare and barren light
    Rob us of our ecstasy?
    Miserere Domine.

The pale moon stares between the trees,
The angry wind has sunk to peace,
Along our lilied terraces.
    Thine eyes are quieted wistfully.
    Miserere Domine.

In the tapestried dark room
Forgotten lies thy silk and loom,
The Gothic casement thro' the gloom
    Sheds the light of sanctity.
    Miserere Domine.

The beacon of the rock is lit:
A growing tower of flame; I sit
Watching the shuddering blaze of it.
    I hear the roaring of the sea.
    Miserere Domine.

Interludes

Ah, love thy hair is sombre gold,
I kiss thee not, lest being bold
My mouth should know thy lips are cold.
   Thy hands droop downward languidly.
   Miserere Domine.

Love itself shall droop and tire,
Life be shorn of all desire,
Passion be a wasted fire
   Gone and perished utterly.
   Miserere Domine.

Ye who have not met with love,
Desire and all the grief thereof,
In your quiet secluded grove
   Holy virgins, pray for me.
   Miserere Domine.

For us who droop with journeying,
With waking and with wearying,
Thro' love and sweet love's languishing.
   God is blind and may not see,
   Miserere Domine.

FATIGUE DU NORD

LO, we are weary of the northern ways:
   Legendary visions of a northern sea:
High carven galleys bound for misty isles
Through hissing foam which sings hypnotically;

Fatigue du Nord

Enchanted mountains peaked and pinnacled,
Spired cities by dim reaches of the sea.

We are grown weary of the flameless nights,
And all the fireless gateways of the day.
We are tormented by old soft delights,
And memories grown bitter as the winds.
These phantom mists have veiled the starry lights
And smothered all the sun-belovèd sky.

Ah! let us seek the blue laburnum blooms
In pleasaunces of honoured Babylon,
Where the dark-purple mulberry juices stain
Rough sepia bark, or leaves of Lebanon,
And where vermilion parrots flash like fire
Thro' aromatic groves of cinnamon.

Come, seek some cloistered orchard filled with fruits:
Sun-bitten peaches plashed with crimson stain,
Wine-laden grapes which shine like jewelled loots
Of drunken armies in surrendered towns,
Or plantains shaped like gold fantastic flutes,
Or odorous mangoes drowsied in the heat.

Flame oranges from Gardens of the Sun,
Light lemons from the Orchards of the Moon,
Bursting pomegranates, shedding rubies red,
Such as some eastern potentate at noon,
Wandering alone upon great garden walls
Had stayed to taste of ere their savours swoon.

Fatigue du Nord

Where life is like a listless paramour
Who groweth wistful as the hot hours wane,
Who melts with sensuous sinking at the hour
When twilight falls upon the burning dial,
While from the incensed heavens like a shower
Descend the flooding miseries of the soul.

Ah! to some holy Opium Garden go,
Where sweet narcotic perfumes fill the air,
And druggèd dreams enfold the passion's woe
With snake-like influences slow and sure,
Where clear herb-scented waters faintly flow
And carmine water-lilies faintly stir.

PETITION

AH, give to me thy pardon, that I bring
So haunted and so sad a heart to thee,
That love's most dear and sweetest comforting
Should come by valley lands of melody
Made musical by rivers of lost tears;
Where each in flowing seems a measured rhyme
Upgathering all the unappeasèd years,
Making a melody of passionate Time.

Yet in the dusk of unaccomplished dreams,
When dews of twilight drench the pallid grass,
And like the sighing of the dead that pass
Wander the silver footfalls of the streams;

Petition

When the white star is caught among the leaves
Of spiritual birch trees wan and frail,
Staring with ashen trunks bedewed and pale
Like ghosts thro'out the many scented eves,

Give me thy pardon and the peace thereof,
With love's strange fervour and the faith of love.

THE ISLAND

ON a half forgotten Island
In a long remembered sea,
High upon the peakèd summit
Stands a towered and domed city,
Which is all possessed by thee.

There the half forgotten colour
Of the drifting evening sea,
Where the crazy-hearted dolphins
Pierce the purple of the billows,
Is alone possessed by thee;

The quiet forsaken harbour,
And the silence of the quay,
Where the crimson cords are twisted
Round the bales and logs of cedar,
Is again possessed by thee;

The Island

The three deserted vessels
In the harbour, restlessly
Straining their high prows, and sighing
With the spirits of the twilight
To be gone across the sea;

The path above the harbour,
Like a snake wound cunningly
Thro' the alleys of the roses,
Past the dew-fed shadowy corners
Of the frail anemone.

The fire-fly laden twilight,
And the amethystine sea,
Where the stars caught in the ocean
Chase the shivering moon of silver:
They are all possessed by thee.

The towers and the turrets,
And the minarets that be
All bejewelled and gold-dusted,
In the long forsaken city
That is looking over sea.

The pallid bronze piazza,
Where shadows tranquilly
Steal across the carven fountain,
Guarded by the fabled griffins
And the horses of the sea.

The Island

The gateways of the Palace
Swinging backward carelessly,
While the sunsets creep and glimmer
Up the coloured Persian carpets
To the throne of ivory.

The golden halls of silence,
And the shaking Judas Tree
Weeping tears of vain repentance,
Dropping blood upon the marble
And the floors of porphyry.

The sword hilts and the scabbards
Set with rubies wondrously,
Scattered in the Council chambers
With the petals of the roses
Which are all possessed by thee.

The terraced almond-gardens,
Where the great sun slantingly
Gilds the sombre row of cypress
Standing gaunt in hollow grandeur
All above the silent sea.

In the blue peaked eastern Island,
The red lantern deathlessly
Lighted by dead hands and holy,
Glimmers in forsaken chambers
And is cast across the sea.

38

The Island

Ah, the pointed purple Island
Which no mariner shall see,
Where no ship shall find a haven,
Where no human love shall wander,
Which is all possessed by thee!

EVENING PARDON

IN the great hush of sunset's ribbèd gold,
   When the vast peace of passion floweth down,
And pardon is possessed a thousandfold
   With slow dew-dropping twilights once our own.

In quiet hours and holy eves when day
   Plays gently on his yielding wizard's strings,
And life draws near to gaze and turn away
   Upon invisible and soundless wings.

As in strange dreams, in silent sacred tides
   The sun thro' amber clouds glows dim and blind,
While rushes gleam like swords on still lake sides,
   And willow leaves turn white against the wind.

In sun-warm gardens soul beloved and dear,
   With idle day-worn petals fallen free,
Pale butterflies in seas of lavender
   Which strive with bumble bees for mastery.

In eventides of love's sweet piety,
   When souls of blessèd tenderness draw nigh,
Shall not the sorrow all forgotten be?
   And blind-eyed wrong be hallowed wonderfully?

For the Beloved

FOR THE BELOVED

NOW will I seek a fabled tower for thee,
   In some belovèd fair-named river way,
Clear refluent and flowing drowsily,
   And sun-flushed in the dying after-day,
Like flowing fire of passion broken free
   Bearing sweet-thoughted reverie away.

There round the island bank with osiers set
   Sway flowery water-plants and whispering weeds,
High golden irises with petals wet,
   And full-starred river-lilies, whose gold seeds
Are spilt like copper dust across roset
   Sweet water-avons by the rusty reeds.

There shall be fairy-glazed smooth marigold,
   And tall grown willow-herb with ruby gleam,
Blue-tinted milk wort, river-saffron cold
   Which swoon upon the pulses of the stream,
Whose waters with soft-handed methods fold
   The yielding water-flowers into a dream.

And round about thy walls black swans shall glide
   For thy fair pleasure all the summer thro',
With blood-red bills and necks of archèd pride,
   And magic rhythmic motion touched with woe,
For they by wicked witchery abide,
   And are sweet princes stolen long ago.

For the Beloved

And these shall thy flower-close incarnadine:
 Deep orange lilies flecked with sable dyes,
And great flame tulips drenched in morning wine,
 While god-begot Adonis-Blossom dies.
And tall fantastic purple columbine
 Which shall thy secret plot imparadise.

And tameless roses shall besiege thy tower
 With riot of sweet sensuous offering,
While in the shining of the sunset-hour
 The roofs blaze yellow where the lichens cling,
And like an amethystine water-shower
 The wild wisterias are wantoning.

Then from the day-fall till the dawn is done,
 Thy twilight turret none shall know, nor see
Thy casement like a fire-lit topaz stone
 With holy arch and carven anciently.
While moonlit loves do make belovèd moan,
 And kissing lips do touch eternity.

THE CITIES OF DESTINY

BY wilderness and flower-enamelled lea,
 And solitudes forsaken of the sea,
Beneath the star-rise and the slow star-wane.

By sun-flushed snow-field and pale water-land,
Towards the faint, far-off, unsounding strand,
To lantern-jewelled cities of the plain;

The Cities of Destiny

By waterless wood-wells and river-beds,
Where sun-beset pale tulips hang their heads,
And rainless willows weep the spray of streams;

Thro' yellow-powdered, bent Mimosa-trees
Heavy with bloom and bowed with reveries,
Dropping gold pollen like the dust of dreams;

Seek we the verges of the twilight plain;
Thro' dark morass and dreary-tracked demesne,
And wizard swamps inhabited of Fear.

While purple poppies shake like violet fire,
And wild hill-roses dewlessly expire
Thro' the belovèd flower-tides of the year.

While golden grapes translucent in the rays
Of dying day-time in the shining days
Light vineyard valleys by unfoaming seas.

Until the star-set till the dusk is done
Like slight gold bubbles fallen from the sun ;
Till they at moonrise shine like treasuries

Of long-dead robbers in forgotten caves
By shores where quiet star-dusted water laves
Along earth's margin all the morning time.

Thro' firefly-lit dim dusk and dewy gloom
Of fairest virgin valleys filled with bloom,
And slopes of amethyst, untrodden thyme;

The Cities of Destiny

Across the pathless plainland shall we go,
With eager spirit and a dream-like woe,
Towards bright cities by lamenting seas.

Where domes and watch-towers as the moonlight pales,
Fair like enchantments of Arabian tales,
Guard fabulous halls and pillared palaces.

There tall magicians on the turrets stand
Gazing across the midnight of the land,
With eyes that glitter with the light of stars.

And there the rumours of strange things go by
Upon the road-winds, while the blossoms fly
With murmurs of the tales of many wars.

And there the criers of the streets, like ghosts,
With visionary eyes, in numbered hosts
Pass by with loud-voiced prophecies of pain.

Up the long single street of each strange town,
Where homeless leaves and buds are vaguely blown,
And shake upon the wind-way all in vain.

From the still plain with unperturbèd feet,
Into the dust-strewn pallor of the street,
With passion-troubled heart and soul-lit eyes.

In vain the holy walls and ways of kings,
In vain the bitterness of love-like things,
Or pensive starry-eyed philosophies!

43

The Cities of Destiny

Thro' the gray sculptured gateway must we go,
Along the red-rose arbours hanging low
Like ruby waterfalls in sunset beams.

Drawn by the shadow of untuned desire,
Led by the leaping of a fuelless fire,
To where is no deliverance from dreams?

PRELUDE

THROUGH the rounded archway where the gate
      hangs loose
Loom the palace gardens shadowed dim,
A cypress, and a porphyry fountain rim
Grown purple in disuse.

Stiff peacocks ruby-eyed in sombre pleasaunces,
Moss-grown avenues where fire-flies glow,
The gate hangs loose, and beckons us to go—
Our pleasure palaced is.

BEATA PAX

A PRIMITIVE PAINTING

WHERE gold-haired kings and grave-eyed Magi
      fill
With colour all the cypress-dusky hill,
By crimson clad and gem-wrought cavalcade,
Which glitters thro' the noonday to the shade,

Beata Pax

Come from mauve hills enchanted by the mist
Of throbbing suns, to palest amethyst;
By flooding rivers flowing from the snows
To sight-lost seas, round isles no galley knows;
By perilled peak and storm-hurt castle wall
Where echoes of the avalanches fall;
Passing down many a forest-shaded vale
Where prisoned winds grow great from pain and wail
Like some divinely-lost divided thing
Made all magnificent thro' sorrowing.
Beside the streams strewn pink with almond bloom
Or Judas tree above a dark rock tomb,
By the anemone-enamelled swards
And pool-reeds set with many shining swords,
By sweet-faced pansies purple with the spring,
And tender swallows weak upon the wing,
Thro' gold-gilt celandine with crystal dew,
And dark-leaved periwinkle white and blue
By sunny spaces kept and comforted;
While lemon coloured butterflies wind-shed,
Assail the fugitive frail cyclamen.
Beside the wayside shrines of wandering men,
Towards the brown hill-cities set with towers,
Mellow beneath the sunshine and the showers.

Ah! might we also pilgrim there, and seek
With heart and feet all trouble-worn and weak
The sun-bronze half forsaken piazza where
Vexed life is stilled from clamour and despair.

45

Beata Pax

Where fragile fountain-water yields like love
Beneath the slight and wayward winds that move
With piteous frequent kisses faint and free
All tremulous with blind-eyed ecstasy :
Like some sweet sudden rage of love unsought,
Beyond all measured moods and ways of thought,
Beyond all counsels of the straining blood
Or secret guarded gateways of the flood;
More pagan-souled than ruby juice run free
From glowing purple grapes crushed wantonly
By slight feet milky-white and violet-veined,
Cool from dark vineyard leaves and purple stained.

Ah, might we, coming to that citadel,
Follow the searching incense like a spell,
To the gold calm of sun-blessed cloister squares
Where some encumbered orange tree still bears
Its heavy fiery fruit, and frescoes pale
From marching summers, linger faint and frail
Above the marble knights effaced and worn;
While worshipping and watchful angels mourn,
Where lily-worked and star-wrought pillars glow
Against the sky all sister like a-row;
And hear the psalmodies of Saints more pure
Than silences of Love grown sweet and sure:
The low-toned songs of those who sweetly sing
The verse of virgins in their ministering :
Spilt melodies from unimpassioned lyres
Made fair thro' far forsaken lost desires.

Beata Pax

And at that shrine of ended pilgrimings
Find certitudes of fond familiar things.
Until each dreamful dusk the sun shall set
On some remembrance of half sweet regret;
Like lips which have bestowed their spells, like eyes
Which have divulged their sweetest mysteries.
As holy-hearted as the reverie
Of some divine and sweet-souled amity
Make full of mercy and a wistful pain
That unapparent pity weeps in vain.
Finding the languor of melodious moods,
And tender calms of sweet solicitudes,
And all pure inspiration born of breath
Made strong and sure beyond the doors of death.
And all the dusk of life and hush of sleep:
Quiet pallors of tired souls who dream and weep.

DREAMERS

WE are become like phantoms of the night
Thro' the heart's pity and the heart's delight.

For we have wandered with the wasting streams
Across the flower-stained solitude of dreams,
The blossom-scattered waterways of dreams.

For we have crossed the lotus-covered lake,
Where only the sunk palaces do shake
Beneath the waters, and the serpents make
A beauteous shining for their passion's sake.

47

Dreamers

Behold, we are like spectres of the night
For the soul's longing and the soul's delight.

Who for dream's pleasure and for love's relief
Have drugged dull Time, the heavy-footed thief
Of the old sorrows and the old belief.

For we are taught the sea's iniquities,
And see, like fearful-thoughted reveries
Sunk vessels by the borders of lost quays.
And pale and dreadful hills below the seas.

Behold, we are the dreams of vanished nights
For old love's anguish and new love's delights.

We are become like lost men on the moon,
Strangers on plains of everlasting noon,
Dread wanderers on the mountains of the moon.

Thus have we seen the moon's dark fortresses
Grown over with the moon-moss, where the trees
Hung with old dews and woeful radiances
Stand like the ghosts of stunted fantasies.

We are dumb phantoms of the hollow night
Thro' the soul's pity and the soul's delight.

First Sorrow

FIRST SORROW

THE first dim morning of your sorrowing,
  The sunrise, O belovèd, of your pain:
Long fingered dawn all unaware shall creep
Upon your soul and wake the pulsèd sleep,
And towards the casement draw your eyes in vain.

The first faint twilight of your travelling:
When the vast afterglow at some wood's end
Holds the world's sorrow, as the pine trees stand
Like warders of the sunset hand in hand,
And thro' the valleys armied shadows wend.

The first desire for long unfettered days,
Which rises with the midnight moon and thrills
The soul upon the morrow morn to hide
Its want with purple plain and waveworn tide,
Or misty cities set on little hills.

When nights and days are one with sorrowing,
May I recount to you all tenderly
The foam-wet roads beside the swinging sea?

A RHAPSODY

"Verse and nothing else have I to give you."

AND now the lantern of thy love shall be
  Like a dead vision come again to me,
For with most lovely fervours once again,

49   E

A Rhapsody

Like the strange vestige of an ancient pain,
Like the lost tumult of a broken lyre
The words shall waken to the heart's desire.

Thy tenderness is like untrodden dew,
Or odorous soft flowers and plaintive rue;
Like dripping unseen fountains in the night,
Or water meadows glimmering to the light;
Like purple hill-lakes where faint islands are
All unattainèd, mystical, afar,
Whither we go not lest its haunted shores
Hold us for ever in bewitched lores,
So that the after life may know no waning
From bitter longing and the soul's complaining.
Thou art to me like some forgotten tune
Heard on the paths of slumber, some lost moon
Perished beneath the sombre hearted days:
Flameless despondencies of winter ways.
Some unconceivèd colour seen in sleep:
A magic radiance wonderful and deep;
For like a starry raiment made to bless,
The spell-bound vision of thy tenderness
Shall lull to lethargy and lassitude
The wasteful woe of the soul's solitude:
The torments, fretful fevers, and dull pain
Bred in the oppressed niches of the brain.

The tide of thy fair tenderness to me
Is like the swaying of a twilight sea,

A Rhapsody

Whose silver dreams and gray far mysteries
Murmur like old undying histories,
Troubling the spirit with strange chorused songs
Of bitter sacrilege and unknown wrongs.

Love's pain is pity and love's pity pain:
Fair glittering blossoms shed like blood in vain,
Passionate Pities, white flames of despair
Parching the soulless silence of the air,
Glowing thro' faith of their own fervencies
Like earth's last sunset over sobbing seas.

Wise Lover of the Pathless Hills! shall I
(Who am more weak and sad than men who die)
Bring torches of the twilight in quiet eves,
Enamelled blossoms and long subtle leaves,
From phantom fens? which to thyself shall seem
The semblance of an idle-hearted dream.

Strong Lover of the Uplands, there may blow
In silent marshes spirit-held and low
Strange blossoms whose fair names enfold the heart
In shadowy morasses far apart:
"Most bitter Moonseed," scattered by pale hands
On moonlight nights across the marshy lands,
Where none may walk for fear of Fantasies,
Or tales of world-old Sorcerers' Savageries.
And there is "Love lies bleeding" red like pain
Which lieth low and may not rise again.

A Rhapsody

And likewise " Love in Languor ", fragile blooms
Clinging across the dampness of young tombs,
Upon the hearts of those who loved too well.
And there is the soul-laden Asphodel,
And "Scattered Stars" and " Tears of Amities,"
And frothy petals from the " Foam of Seas ";
" Fire of Few," Samphire and "Wanderer's Sorrow,"
And Fireflies of the night-time and the morrow
Which are waste passions of enamoured souls
Crowning the dusky flowers like aureoles.
And there are silver places sunnier
Than Paradise, and irised meres more fair
Than heaven's water-lands, and there the plot
Of " Spirit Need " or " Love remembered not."
And here across the misty day-fall go
Will-o'-the-wisp moving in measure slow,
And thro' the throbbing of the amorous night
Seeking the flame-flies for their fair delight;
And here are shining dragon-flies caressing
The starlight on dark water, half possessing,
And moaning moths with jewel-entangled wings
That may not fold or fly from languishings.

What shall Love give since Love must give to thee?
Fair pictures fashioned to a melody:
Cool Persian Lilacs by gray mountain ways,
Or Fuchsia Forests in the flaming days?
All the torn tumult of a broken lyre,
Which are pale phantoms of the heart's desire?

Flight

FLIGHT

MIRABELLE has fled away,
  Over lands low-lying,
In the dew-time of the day
  When the day is dying.

Over lake and river-land,
  Sad and spirit-laden,
To the sand-dunes and the strand,
  And the windless haven;

Where the long ships lie at rest
  All the early dawning,
With their black prows to the west
  Till the tidal warning.

While the lights upon their sides
  Shake across the river,
Leaping on the inky tides
  Like fiery snakes that quiver.

Till the full tide laps and lulls
  Round the wharfs and rafters,
And the shadows of the hulls
  Stain the swaying waters.

Mirabelle has fled away
  Thro' the misty marches,
Where the wind-lutes lilt and play,
  Round the ghostly larches.

Flight

Through the willows of the dawn
  Sighing in the shadows,
With her soul shut she has gone
  Past the magic meadows.

Coming to the carven ships,
  With their topsails sighing,
By the wharf-sides and the slips
  As the day was dying.

To the battered brigs that go
  Through the swinging oceans,
O'er the green sea to and fro
  With mesmeric motions;

Reaching garden-lands that lie
Full of gracious reverie
  In the violet mountains,
Where the rainbow butterfly
  Flecks the flower-grown fountains.

Where enamoured stars down-rain
Love-struck to the earth again
  On the evening alleys,
And the blue grapes droop and wane
  In the verdant valleys.

*   *   *   *   *   *

She has fled through marshes cold
  From her turret chamber:
Mirabelle with head of gold
  Touched with fiery amber!

REINCARNATION

I

ANOTHER life, another span is come;
  Shall it be said that what He has decreed
Is strong against the face of our great need
That what we were we may no more become?
Ah love, if it should be that in this birth
I do not find thee thro' the circling days,
But sing for evermore a passion's praise,
And go unhearkened to the waiting earth;
Then will I pray one prayer to Him above,
For one celestial vision to foretell
That life and love are ours, that love is well—
So shall we find fulfilment to our love,
And the long sorrow of a myriad years
Be hallowed by the harvest of our tears.

II

Ah love, my love, is thy remembrance strong?
Does thy strange dual soul remember yet
The vast emotions that our lives beget,
Or is the circle of the years too long?
Hast thou forgot, and dost no longer know
The gray North seas, the tossing spray, the cry
Of our great love wrung out in agony,
The swaying prows against the afterglow?

Reincarnation

Ah love, my love, thou shalt remember soon
The fierce denial of law, the deep desire,
The crimson sunset like a sheet of fire
The oarsmen swinging to a ballad tune.
Ah love, my love, is thy remembrance strong?
It is so long ago, it is so long!

III

Shalt thou behold me with a faint surprise,
As at the vision of a dear face lost,
Or the wan image of a dead friend's ghost?
Till our past life rise up before thine eyes:
A sea-girt castle tower where mournfully
The waves arise and fall thro'out the day,
Casting aloft their milky showers of spray;
The iron-barred casement facing the dim sea
Which moves beneath the moonlight faint and fair;
The crimson raiment round thy body's grace,
The dreams that veil the passion of thy face,
The fillet in thy aureole of hair;
A brazier's incense mounting thro' the gloom,
The wave-bound silence of a turret-room.

IV

Thou light of mine, we may not tell of this
To other men, but each alone goes forth
On all the hollow days to South or North,
Weeping at pain and wondering at bliss;
Until some strain of melody expands,

Reincarnation

And fires the dormant longing, and we see
Stealing across the soul's infinity
An echo of our fair Sicilian lands.
Ah, love of mine, how may we well forget
Our faint blue island our Hesperides
Washed by the silver foaming of the seas?
Not all this life shall teach us to forget
The sapphire seas, the amethyst wild seas
Chanting their magical monotonies.

Twilight Seas

TWILIGHT SEAS

BY twilight seas when the great harvest moon
    Arises from the ocean, floating wide
In skies a misty purple either side,
Cry loud to Death and bid him follow soon!
For lo! along the sea a burnished road
Of copper gold is thrown, where ripples red
Flow fast in wizard light, and white stars shed
Full on dark waters half their silver load.

Pass down in peace to where that widening way
In golden foam laps low on answering shores,
And as ebb-tide swings back magnetic doors,
Float down the path, on molten billows sway
Towards the moon, while the pale fingers fling
Great showers of fiery drops that hiss and sting.

Fairy Lands

FAIRY LANDS

IN fabulous riverlands of imagery,
  Some ancient wizard crones beside the streams,
And weaves with furrowed hands the web of dreams,
Beating slow time to tunes of fantasy;
There grape-encumbered purple towers stand,
Whilst o'er the wine-red plains of evening
The wild flamingoes homeward westering
Move like a crimson cloud across the land.

And dragons emerald-scaled, asleep o' nights
In vaporous forests, hear the hollow tramp
Of war-horses, and see the gold-eyed lamp
Throw its long glint along the spears of knights,
Who to the mighty slaying silent creep,
That gold-haired maidenhood may quiet sleep.

Graves

GRAVES

DIG slow the grave of Love if dead he be,
 Beside the water-way, beneath the hill,
Where winds sweep not and all the grass is still,
Save where faint harebells rustle tenderly.
 For no man walks along the river-side
Where wave the willow trees below the curve,
There the great waters eddy sweep and swerve;
 Ere languidly they wander to the tide.

Dig deep the grave of Love if slain he be,
 Set there a cross, nor linger near to weep,
 But pray that all his slumber may be deep,
That for Love's sake he may forgotten be.

Yet shall the slayer pass some silent day
And stumble on the cross with eyes astray.

Willow Lore

WILLOW LORE

THE spectre willows over the fair streams,
  Ghost-gray and frail with silver whisperings,
Forbid the way across the fen of dreams,
For awe of their inconstant murmurings.
So white are they, so pale and wonder-wan,
So full of wizard words and virginal
Wind-woven flutings, that their mournful tone
Weaves a faint spell of stories magical.

Ah, who shall ever lose the willow lore
Who once has heard it on the even time?
Ah, who may pass the stream-lands any more,
Whilst all the long leaves swing to water-rhyme?
So strange are they, so drooping and so wan,
So passionless and pale, so woebegone.

Midnight Landscape

MIDNIGHT LANDSCAPE

MINE eyes look out to thee across the night,
  In wooded denes too dark for shadows roam
The hollow murmurs of the prisoned storm;
Full on the river's bend the uncertain light,
Diffused from some invisible moon or star
Shines like the haunted glow of willowed swamps;
The city streets in lines of windy lamps
Across the low dark land wink fast and far.

Forlorn night owls hoot faintly from the tower;
Bats wheel their flight thro' fine wind-driven rain;
The bare black hills crouch low like things in pain
Beneath the living midnight's awful power.
Towards the East, beyond the reach of tears,
Thine eyes look back to me across the years.

Autumn

AUTUMN

THE paling autumn sunlight, lean and stark,
   Throws lengthening lances thro' the cedar tree,
Finds out the emerald down on branch and bark
And sinks on rivers flowing easefully.
At evening pass across the plain where stands
The tawny beech tree on the little rise,
While sunset spreads abroad his glowing hands,
And quivering leaves are frail on golden skies.

There sound the deer herds thro' the fallen leaves
Like phantom souls of lovers trooping past:
Thro' all the world, thro' all the sorrowing eves
They wander till they find their peace at last.

Love, if amongst these dead perchance you be,
Ah, fling awide your heart and call to me!

Death

.   .

DEATH

IF I should never come, beloved, to thee,
　But wander with the same unflowing tears
Down all the long and labyrinthine years
Wherethro' the footfalls echo audibly.
When death draws near me shall I lie and see
The vision of thy face, as one who hears
After long darkness and slow fallen fears
The faint accomplishment of melody?

Beside a casement open to the sky,
Whilst flaming evening sinks upon the world,
Stains the whole land to palest emerald,
Lights all the hills and waits to see me die.

Ah, Love receive at last the dying sigh:
"So did I never find thee in the world."

Love's Eternity

LOVE'S ETERNITY

I

MY Lover, we are strong we shall not die,
   Yet may we never whisper nor impart
What lies in the recesses of the heart,
Nor how we love nor why we cannot die.
Yet see, thy hand alone is stronger far
Than all the generations of high things:
Purer than sacred battles of great kings,
More holy than Christ's city seen afar.

Thou hast the soul of fire which men of old
Painted between sweet prayers and holy names
On heaven's blue dusk, beside a scroll of gold,
Recording pious deeds and goodly fames.
Bright flame of God upon the evening sky,
Which upward burneth and can never die.

II

The years shall hold our love when life shall go,
So strong are they, and love is small and weak,
Therefore the patient years shall bid love speak
With accents sure and meditation slow.
Some murmur of this tale shall wander forth
And mix its message with a winter wind,
Drive joy away and leave sweet peace behind.
Our love shall travel to the South and North,

Love's Eternity

Fair tales shall tell our love when life is fled,
Sweet hallowed songs shall sing our grief to men,
Our dear delight shall live when we are dead;
Else grief had been as desolate as when
One cometh to cross-roads beneath the moon,
Where laden gallows swing against the sky!

III

Love, we will cast a spell upon the wind
Like wizards of old time, and bid him keep
This tale of tears thro' all his time of sleep
To tell in days of storm to humankind.
Love, we will bid him whisper to the trees
Upon the barren hill-tops of the world,
And pipe loud wonders where the waves are hurled,
And fill the moonrise and the dusk with peace.
He shall command and teach the silver wells
Unknown and hidden in the hills of thyme,
To sing our passion till the end of time.
Love, he shall wander with magician spells
Unto the chambers of sweet lovers dead,
And breathe love's comfort round the fallen head.

IV

Love, we will tame the voices of the sea,
Teach the great rivers and enslave the floods
Which wander thro' the flowerless solitudes
To tell of love and love's eternity.
So that the dwellers of the pathless plain,

68

Love's Eternity

Hearing the waters of the spring shall say:
"Hear now the singing ones that come our way
Full of spring joyance and the fallen rain.
They tell of grief, we know not whence they flow,
They sing of love, we know not where they go,
They tell of love and love's eternity.
Lo, love is all we have, and love is dear,
And death the vanquisher is not so near
But that we shall escape him utterly!"

Dear Saint

DEAR SAINT

I

DEAR Saint, I may not minister to thee,
Like some poor sinner of an ancient rime,
Nor kiss thy wounds with fervour time on time,
Nor woo away thy slightest agony.
Sweet Saint, I may not touch thy dearest head
With loving lips, lest all my soul should guess
Thy longing and despair and loneliness,
And hope which may not linger being dead.

Belovèd Saint, I may not sing to thee,
Lest music overflow with love and pity,
And make too sweet and passionate a ditty;
I may not bring incense or thyme to thee,
Or burn gold flames before thee circlewise,
Who art adorable and dear and wise.

II

Now would I seek the comfort of thine eyes,
And beg the comfort of thy hands to hold,
And pray thy counsel clear and gentle-wise
Sweet Friend, to shield me from the outer cold.
But lo, thy soul is bountiful to bless,
And should my sorrow murmur unto thee,
Sweet fervour would disturb thy tenderness
For pity of my soulful malady.

Dear Saint

And ah! it were not well, it were not well
To shade the risen sunlight of thy peace,
Tho' all life's pain were rendered tolerable
By the acceptance of thy comfort's ease,

Tho' grief itself should grow beloved and dear,
Sweet Friend, to know thy consolation near.

Lament

LAMENT

"Down in yonder greene field
There lies a knight slain under his shield."

I

I DARE no longer dream of asphodel
In emerald pastures by forgetful streams,
Since thy fair face is grown invisible
I may no longer broider death with dreams:
I dare no more behold the west wind pass,
With blown white poplar flowers beside the sea,
Strewing the margin of the meadow grass
Upon the strand of dark Persephone.

Lest I behold thee by the water-side
Shrouded in everlasting eventide.

No Saint was e'er so beautiful as thou,
No martyr half so passionate or free,
No knight of legend had so pure a brow,
No sad-souled poet had the eyes of thee!

II

Through dying evenings now do I perceive
Thy face as that of some belovèd knight
Sung of in battle, or by fires at night
Where waiting women sit and slowly weave

72

Lament

Their grief into the labours of their hands.
I do possess thee as the jewelled tale
Of one fair knight who desolate and pale
Subdued the perils of the wooded lands.

And when the night is come I do behold
Thy face as that of some enshrinèd saint
Dead long ago, which vanished hands did paint
Upon a background set about with gold.
Thus when the night is come thou art not dead,
Nor can I look upon thee wearièd.

À sa Dame

À SA DAME

AH Sweet, behold me with thy gentlest eyes,
  Although I lay small tribute at thy feet,
For love is all that I may give my Sweet.
Behold I would thy sweetness sanctuarize
Until all sinners pray beside thy shrine,
And all the lonely-hearted come to thee
To lose their sorrows for a reverie,
And leave their longing for the hope of thine.

Sweet Heart, behold me with dear charity,
And give thy pardon if my weak distress
Should seem too sad a part of tenderness,
And joy grow saddened for the love of thee.

Dear, though I lay all life beneath thy feet,
Yet love is all that I may give my Sweet.

Burden

BURDEN

" BEHOLD the burden of the soul shall grow
  To be so great a load upon this time,
And its deep longing waxen so sublime,
That the whole world must surely feel its woe."
So sang I once, I may not love thee now,
Nor may I speak of sorrow, for indeed
Of late thou seemest dumb in thy great need,
And my poor sighs were sacrilege enow.

I have not wept enough to worship thee,
And idle were the tears I deemed divine,
Within the holy silence of thy shrine
The wells of sorrow are too pure for me.
May I draw near albeit wearily,
When I have languished long and wept for thee?

Remorse

REMORSE

A Sonnet Sequence

I

THAT you should cast away so poor a thing;
Look back upon the past with careless ease,
Nor let the lurking whisper of the trees
Break thro' your peace with a strange murmuring!
Yet in the torpid years of youth's decay,
When spirits shall arise in multitude
And drive your joy away in battle rude
Beyond the purple distances of day;

Then shall you stay, as I have stayed, to see
The light die from the world at even-close?
Whilst o'er green river-lands of fair repose
The wild black swans fly homeward wearily;
And hear the tree-tops' tell-tale whispering:
"How did you cast away so poor a thing?"

II

Watch not the great gold moon like heaven's lamp
Rise in the night above the water way,
And light returning ships; the sea-worn Tramp,
The battered brigs that have been long away,
With salten sails agilt like glowing wings
Gilded again upon the hushèd waves,
Rejoicing that they cease their wanderings,

Remorse

And hear no more the criers of the graves
That in the watery deeps forgotten lie.

Watch not alone, lest thro' the soul of you
The vessels pass like moving imagery,
And the long pageant of a life renew;
Watch not the ships glide home to harbouring,
Lest you should half regret so poor a thing.

III

Nor lie awake with weary dream-worn brain
In the great cities thro' the morning time,
Where muffled sounds of sorrow undermine
The splashing of the unrelenting rain.
Where thro' the awful silence of the street
Comes one forsaken footfall drawing nigher,
Mounting and growing like a live desire
To sink away with far receding feet.

Across the infinite star-laden sky
Hear not the dirges of the quick and dead
Bridging the gulf of time with surging tread,
As measured funerals of the years go by;
Lest thro' the lulls the beating rhythms ring:
"How did you cast away so poor a thing?"

IV

Watch not in dull hours feverish and outworn
The singing nettles on the ruined wall,
Whilst thro' the vaporous forest-glooms forlorn
The autumn rains on sodden beech-leaves fall.

Remorse

Nor watch hill-peaks against the afterglow
Strange, mystical, and waning oversoon,
Waiting behind earth's barriers to throw
Its dying glory on the rising moon.

Pass on! nor listen to the long wind's cry
Across the barren fir-trees and the snow,
Nor hear the footfalls of the world go by,
As dying children heard them long ago.
Cry not across the fateful evening:
"How did I cast away so poor a thing?"

v

Ah, wander not alone on windy nights
Thro' long forsaken corridors and rooms,
Where restless dust lies hidden in the glooms,
And mantled bats wheel blind and aimless flights;
Lest on some rattling casement rough and old
The spirits of the storm should hurl their hate,
And fling their ire with wailing desperate
For disbelief and calumnies untold.

Nor sit within your chamber musingly,
With the low taper dying by degrees,
Lest loud against the window-pane the trees
Should knock their tell-tale hands, till suddenly
You cry upon the tempest's entering:
"Well did I crush so pitiful a thing!"

After Death

AFTER DEATH

IF thou shouldst come to me when I am dead,
Across the mournful all-dividing sea,
Bright browed, and stand beside the tapered bed
To watch the still flame burning steadily:
Then kiss me on the brows for amity,
Sweet amity forsaken and unblessed;
And on the lips for sorrows' remedy,
And on the eyes for fervours unpossessed.

Then stay beside me for a little while,
But do not linger lest I wake from sleep
Thro' pain of thine indifference if thou smile,
And pity of thy sorrow if thou weep.
If thou shouldst come to me when I am dead
Across the mournful all-dividing sea!

To ——

TO ——

"My public, my critic, and my fame."

WIND instruments of rosy almandine,
    And carven flutes for many gales have I,
And sweet-toned choric dulcimers divine
To tell of faith and passion's psaltery.
And yet no wind bud-laden shall arise
Full of the sound of water and lost leaf,
To strike the strings and fully melodize
The tender fervour and the sweet belief.

And flowers of many pastures have I known:
Heliotrope swooning of its own perfume,
And miles of crimson clover are mine own,
Which sun and stars alternately illume
For pleasure of the soul, and yet for me
No song grows perfect that is made for thee.

On a Bust of Queen Mary I

ON A CONTEMPORARY MARBLE BUST
OF QUEEN MARY I

I WATCH thy deathless sorrow day by day,
  And see the mists of morning in thy soul
Sink down and grapple and possess thee whole.
I see thee as a ghost forlorn and gray,
With haggard eyes that may not cease to see,
Whilst long undying sunsets glow and move
Across the pallid burden of thy love.
Lady, I see thee face infinity
Thro'out the unrelenting centuries;
I watch the cruel years like iron hands
Possess thy peace, as some old foe demands
The buried corpses of thy memories.
Almost I see the murdered paradise
Within the marble prison of thine eyes.

Spring

SPRING

SO would I bid thee come in the fair spring,
Upon a time of daffodils awet
With diamond rains, of celandines gold-set
In emerald moist meadows, wherethro' sing
The crystal streams that go a-wandering
And murmur of their joyance as they fret
The red-earth banks where grows love's amulet:
Rose-tinted wind-flowers frail and quivering.

So would I bid thee come upon a day
Of sun-warm wind when all the cherry-trees
Shed scented snows with smooth uncounting ease;
That thou mayst kiss my lips and haste away
With love and me upon this happy day,
Nor wonder any more of destinies.

Vision

VISION

ACROSS the waste of years I saw thy face:
As one who comes across familiar hills
Forgetful of their beauty, till a space
Of sorrowing thought encompass him, which fills
His soul with sight of all that he has lost;
So that the river-lands beneath his feet
Seem a far vision of the uttermost
Deep wonderment, where soul and silence meet.

Across the waste of dreams I saw thine eyes,
And knew them for the light I once had known:
As poplar trees, wind-blown against the skies,
To prisoners freed, bring joy which shall atone
For all the tears, for all the iron days,
Tall poplar trees along the waterways!

Divided Lands

DIVIDED LANDS

IN the soul's sanctum shalt thou think of it?
   Musing upon the way I love thee so,
With neither awe nor wonderment, albeit
It cometh as a sacred nuncio
From holiest places where no man may go.
And shall the lost years seem a hollow thing
To wonder on a little mournfully:
A land of pilgrim paths and travelling,
A valley of great rivers never free
To cleave the hills and reach the singing sea.

Shall life be as two lands where we may see
The further as a place of wandering:
A starless plain where trooping shadows go,
And our soul's peace the line dividing it?

Pine Woods

PINE WOODS

THE fiery fingers of the sunset thrust
A slanting radiance thro' the sombre pines,
Which stains their roughened bark to iron rust
And the quiet silver pool incarnadines.
Beyond the glowing trunks where hot winds pass
Shines forth a space of flowers, where tawny broom
Tosses faint shadows over sun-gilt grass
And blazes to a flame-begotten bloom.

The last winds of the sunset rise and sweep
Thro' all the forest like a roaring sea,
We shall no more lament nor may we weep,
For lo, our love is blessèd wondrously.
Ah, stay and hear this tumult from above:
The chanting of the choristers of love.

Dusk

.

DUSK

WHAT can they know of love who know not thee?
Nor can they tell of dreams who dream not so.
Ah, turn thy poet-face towards the glow
Of the red fire dying dreamily.
I watch the sapphire dusk, the poplar tree
Against the mystic blue moves to and fro,
I hear the wind of twilight come and go
Across our lily-garden fitfully.

I turn and watch the copper firelight gleam
Within the hallowed mystery of thine eyes,
Of late so tender and so wonder-wise,
So strong in their desire, that they seem
A quiet abode of holy Paradise,
Staying awhile the passion for the dream.

Night

NIGHT

AH love, the yearning of our souls shall pass;
  Now may we with our silence seek and say
The words that haunt our hearts thro'out the day.
Now may we linger on the dew-drenched grass
While oleanders stir across the moon,
And with the moonlit lilies white and wan
Dream that we hear the magic need of Pan
Await the nightingale that cometh soon.

And in the unity of love's delight
Murmur of how we lived and loved of yore
With the great lovers of dim legendary lore;
Upon the sweet approaching of the night
Fling wide the doors and bid the soul go free
Upon its amorous infinity.

Intercessio Poetarum

INTERCESSIO POETARUM

RING the Aves thro' the eve
From cathedrals gray and gold,
When still maidens wait and weave;
For us the solitary-souled.

Chant the metred requiem,
Like the pulse of the departed
Clamouring in the churchyard dim;
For us the lonely-hearted.

When within the fane ye pray
For a holy benison,
At the setting of the day
Kneel ye down in unison.

In the twilight sanctuaries,
By the ruby-studded panes,
Beg for sweet tranquillities,
As the stone-gray daylight wanes.

In the faint cathedral dusk
When the passing bell shall ring,
Burn the incense sweet as musk,
For our sorrow's comforting.

Intercessio Poetarum

Take the tapers tall and bright,
Set them by the Virgin shrine,
Burning in the heart of night,
   For a fervour vespertine.

Tell your holy rosaries
With the first star white and cold,
For our soul's faint maladies;
   We the solitary-souled:

Intercede lest we should seek
(Faint and desolate are we!)
With heart's want and longing weak
   Some divinest amity.

Chant the prayer for passion's peace,
Making quietful melody,
Bring our torment to its ease,
   Miserere Domine!

Intone for us the sinner's chant,
Hymn the psalm and chant the rites,
Lest we die of lover's want
   In the early blossomed nights.

Bring the Sainfoin pure and sweet,
Wet from cristal meadow springs,
Blown where sinuous stream-ways meet
   Thro' the dew-bright evenings:

Intercessio Poetarum

Starry from the river-spray,
Carmine-flushed and budded full,
Scented like the Holy Hay
   Blooming for a miracle.

For our sorrow's sanctity
Offer this by altars old
Of your gracious charity!
   For us the solitary-souled.

Milton Keynes UK
Ingram Content Group UK Ltd.
UKHW022355041223
433798UK00005B/169

9 781019 618806